HANDMADE

HOW EIGHT EVERYDAY PEOPLE BECAME

ARTISAN FOOD ENTREPRENEURS

AND THEIR RECIPES FOR SUCCESS

JENNIFER LEWIS

COPYRIGHT © 2012 BY JENNIFER LEWIS

PUBLISHED BY RABBIT RANCH PUBLISHING

ISBN 13: 978-0615615837

ISBN 10: 061561583X

EDITOR TAMARA MILLER HOPP

COVER PHOTOGRAPHY MARTHA LARSON

COVER DESIGN MICHELLE DRAEGER

Other Small Food Business Books

 Starting A Part-time Business: Everything You Need To Know To Turn Your Passion For Food Into A Successful Business Without Necessarily Quitting Your Day Job

 Food On Wheels: The Complete Guide To Starting A Food Truck, Food Cart, Or Other Mobile Food Business

Join the Small Food Business conversation at www.smallfoodbiz.com.

To Sam & Wendi for giving food entrepreneurs

a place to make their dreams come true.

Find something you love to do

and you'll never have to work a day in your life.

~Harvey MacKay

TABLE OF CONTENTS

INTRODUCTION

Everyone loves a good rags-to-riches story, don't they?   Reading about how someone who started with nothing more than a simple roadside lemonade stand at age 8 and became the leading lemonade producer in the country gives us all hope that we, too, can create something spectacular from nothing more than our vision and dreams. The problem with those magazine and online articles about successful entrepreneurs is that they often take you from the start of the company – those humble beginnings – directly to the end without showing you what the entrepreneur did in the "middle."

Like most people, I was wooed by these articles and seduced into thinking that starting an artisan food business was a way to create a brand and a company I could believe in. Fresh from an MBA program and with a pastry arts degree in my back pocket, I was confident that I had the necessary skills to get my own vision up and running without a problem. Truth be told, I did get it up and running, but then came the "middle" part of my company's story – the part no one ever tells you about - and it was filled with doubts, questions and unforeseen circumstances. My pastry arts degree had prepared me well for the culinary production aspect of the business and my MBA had prepared me for the business planning, marketing strategy, and financial expertise that running the company demanded. But I was a bit at a loss when it came to the specific day-to-day decisions, things like how to develop packaging that matched the vision in my head as well as my limited budget. Or whether a certain social media tool was the right way to communicate with my customers and would help grow my business into the empire I dreamed of.

Luckily for me, my business was located in a kitchen incubator where multiple food entrepreneurs shared the space. So, while waiting for my treats to bake or while washing dishes, I'd talk with the other entrepreneurs and pick their brains. I learned about what they were doing, what had worked for them, and what mistakes they had made. As an artisan food entrepreneur, this type of network proved to be a much more valuable guide when navigating that "middle" part than any magazine article. I believe that was in part because these people, like me, were focused exclusively on the food industry, which comes with its own unique set of rules, regulations and bureaucracies. These entrepreneurs also didn't have large bank accounts to bankroll their endeavors or angel investors and venture capitalists knocking on their doors offering them boatloads of money. In an artisan food business, every single dollar and decision is critical. There's no budget for large focus groups, not enough staff for massive media campaigns or large-scale distribution. So learning from one another helped each of us map out our own path to success.

Because this type of information had been so valuable to my own business' success, when I wrote my first food business book, *Starting A Part-time Food Business*, I included several short interviews from other food entrepreneurs. I wanted to help those who were just starting a food business understand some of the ups and downs inherent with becoming a food entrepreneur. The feedback I've received since that book was published has been that readers found those interviews to be incredibly helpful. As such, the idea for this book was born. The goal of this book is to provide more in-depth case studies with food artisans who, like most of us, don't come armed with millions of dollars with which to start their business. These entrepreneurs started with a driving passion for the product they make and a commitment to producing something unique and, in many cases, made completely by hand. These case studies also aim to show what these entrepreneurs did, on a tactical and strategic basis, to grow their customer base and, ultimately, their sales revenue.

Obviously, everyone's business idea, competitive environment, and access to resources are different. But I hope that by learning what's worked for others, you will gain the inspiration necessary to start your own small food business -- or some guidance and ideas as you work your way through your own "middle."

Talking with Mari Luangrath, whose open and engaging manner automatically puts people at ease, it's hard to imagine such a spirited person initially choosing a career that requires solitude in order to excel. Mari is a quintessential people-person which may help explain why her original career ambition to become a professional violinist never became a reality. What she never could have imagined though, was that this kitchen novice would start what has turned into the most popular cupcake delivery business in the greater Chicago area.

Mari first picked up a violin at age 2 and was rarely without it growing up. "For as long as I could remember I wanted to be a musician," Mari says. "That's what everyone expected me to do." Mari dedicated hours every day to fine-tuning her skills. It seemed like all that hard work was paying off when she was awarded a music scholarship to college, but two years into the grueling bachelor's program Mari realized that music was not the right career path for her. While she adored music, Mari found the hours of practice lonely and isolating. This extrovert needed to be with people.

"When I realized that [I no longer wanted to focus on music], I literally just picked a major on the other side of campus so I wouldn't have to see the music building anymore," Mari says, explaining how she ended up graduating with a major in international relations. Mari figured her major would prepare her for a future law career. But life took yet another detour as she later walked out of the law school entrance exam (LSAT) when it dawned on her in the middle of the test her heart wasn't really into becoming a lawyer. "You could say I had a bit of a career identity crisis for 25 years," Mari says with a laugh.

It would be a mistake to call Mari lazy, though. Like many new college graduates, she simply didn't know what she wanted to do with her life. You don't make it to her level as a violinist without having an incredibly high level of drive and ambition though so idly staying home was never an option she considered. Unfortunately, Mari's husband had a job that made it difficult for Mari to hold down a career. They moved six times in as many years for his work, leaving Mari with a resume that included a mish-mash of work experience: stints as a legal assistant, a food buyer, and a public relations professional. Mari also started two companies on her own during this time – a wholesale stamping distribution company that imported supplies into the U.S. for scrapbook retailers and a home staging business in 2004 when the real estate market was red hot.

It wasn't until Mari, now a mother, was settling into life in the suburbs of Chicago after yet another move when she hit on the idea of starting a cupcake business. The idea actually came to her while struggling to get a bakery to deliver cupcakes to her house for an event. There were cupcakes stores throughout downtown Chicago, but none were willing to deliver to the suburbs for less than $150. "Foiled Cupcakes really came about because I saw a problem and wanted to solve it," Mari says.

Realizing that she couldn't possibly be the only person in the suburbs who'd faced this issue before, Mari decided that she wanted to start a cupcake company that, unlike most others in the area, wouldn't have a storefront. Instead it would focus solely on delivering delicious cupcakes for reasonable prices. Today, Foiled Cupcakes gives Chicago-area cupcake-lovers the ability to order cupcakes in an array of decadent and imaginative flavors and have them delivered to their front door the very next day. "The only way we could keep the cost of delivery low was if we didn't have a 100,000-square-foot, $10,000-per-month, storefront lease that we also had to pay for," Mari says.

Since Foiled Cupcakes are delivered, a minimum order of a dozen cupcakes is required. "I didn't want to sell individual cupcakes," Mari explains. "When I was doing research for this company it seemed like every time I walked by a cupcake store there would be someone sitting by themselves eating a cupcake with tears streaming down their face like they were trying to drown their sorrows in the frosting. I didn't want my cupcakes to be a sad experience for anyone. The minimum dozen order means that the cupcakes are going to be shared and are usually ordered for birthdays, weddings, and office parties." Though the order minimum is 12 cupcakes, Mari says that the average order size is closer to seven – eight dozen.

Here's the interesting part of this business plan, though – Mari doesn't have the slightest bit of a culinary background. She is the first to admit that her kitchen competency is far below what's respectable, so the idea of starting up a cupcake business was almost laughable. Except that Mari is not someone who lets anything stand in her way. "I asked my best friend from high school, who is a trained pastry chef, to come out to Illinois and teach me how to bake," Mari says. "She trained me on food science, basic baking, food preparation, and how to manage large-scale production." This friend helped Mari create the recipes and then wished her luck in the new venture before returning to California.

Mari believes that her initial lack of baking skills actually worked to her advantage because it prompted her to realize that she needed to hire good bakers to create the quality product she wanted her company to be known for. Mari sought out bakers and pastry professionals who would be able to easily work with the recipes she'd created. It turns out that hiring people she trusts to do the culinary work also frees Mari up to focus more of her energies on the marketing and branding of Foiled Cupcakes. "All cupcakes are basically sugar, butter, and eggs," Mari says pointedly. The challenge was finding a way to make her cupcakes stand out from every other cupcake store in Chicago.

To achieve this, Mari once again relied on others to help her. In this case she brought together a highly skilled branding team that included a graphic designer, copywriter, and web designer. Knowing that she wanted her company to be associated with fun (no crying in the cupcakes!), Mari worked closely with this group to develop a brand for the company that was in line with the look and feel Mari wanted her business to exude. Mari believes that this was some of the best money she spent in the initial phases of her business' growth because that team of experts was able to create a brand personality that guides all other marketing decisions.

For example, every Foiled Cupcake comes with what is called a "Quippie." These inedible adornments, attached to the top of the cupcake with frosting, have a whimsical saying on it that acts as a conversation starter or ice breaker. Though most cupcake companies eschew adding anything inedible to their products, Mari and her team believe the addition of Quippies are very much in line with the brand they were trying to create. Mari recalled her own days of working in corporate environments and that whenever anyone would bring in cupcakes to the office everyone would grab their cupcake and then return to their desk. "I wanted our cupcakes to facilitate communication and be fun for people," Mari explains. The Quippies have been so successful that in addition to having different Quippies for different themes, such as birthdays, bridal showers, or office parties, Foiled Cupcakes are often asked to create custom Quippies with logos for corporate events or to send as client gifts.

In addition to the Quippies, a large part of Foiled Cupcakes' success can be attributed to Mari's social media strategy, though she'd be the first to tell you that it's less strategy and more an organic outgrowth of who she is and what the company stands for. "Social media and being social is an extension of my personality," she says, remembering that she left the music program at school because it was too isolating. "Being social from behind a computer while running a business and answering phone calls is a natural fit." She doesn't consider her approach to social media to be strategic, per se, but she approached it with the business mind of a true marketer. Mari first started by making sure she understood who her customers were, in part by talking to customers who placed orders to learn more about them and their needs. Based on that and some other demographic research, she was able to pinpoint that her company's main customer base was women ages 18-40 who lived in the Chicagoland area. "I tried to figure out what else all these women would have in common and I realized that almost all women love shoes and chocolate!"

With that, Mari started doing Twitter searches for people who met her customers' demographic profile and who were talking about shoes and/or chocolate. "I would find those people and develop a relationship with them through the conversations we had about shoes or chocolate," Mari explains. "It's not a strategy; we just started to connect with people about things we could talk about. I can't talk to you in any great depth about global warming, but I can talk to you about a sale at Banana Republic!" Mari is genuine in her online friendships and works hard to build a community regardless of if they will ever purchase cupcakes from her. "So many small businesses are trying to find ways to pitch their business and promote themselves that it can turn into their downfall," Mari says. "A lot of people are turned off by that. What people want are genuine good people who they can trust and they won't trust you until they know you are human. You have to show them that you have a human side and a personality outside of your company."

In fact, Mari rarely mentions her company in social media conversations as her focus is on building those personal relationships. She has learned that as people get to know her and trust her they are much more willing to purchase cupcakes from her too. "I think the reason we were able to get the word out so quickly about Foiled Cupcakes was because of social media, but the success really came from the fact that we spent time creating a genuine community of people so that when our website was ready, the orders started piling in quickly."

Mari's focus on community-building doesn't stop with the computer. Through social media, she was able to create such a dedicated and connected following that Foiled Cupcakes started a group that brings online friends together for dinner, called Sushi Club by Foiled. And, upon learning that many of their online friends loved running, Foiled Cupcakes partnered with the largest running shoe company in Chicago to hold runs and races that end with everyone enjoying beer and cupcakes. "It's doing fun stuff with people – being part of the community," Mari says enthusiastically. "Hopefully people will talk with us online or take part in our events and tell their friends that we have the best cupcakes but we like doing these things that show that we're not all about cupcakes. We care about community and we want to use our cupcakes to build community."

As much as she loves dedicating time to social media, it's equally important for Mari to disconnect each day and spend quality time with her husband and son. Like working mothers everywhere, the biggest challenge Mari has is finding enough time to get everything done without feeling like anything or anyone is being shortchanged. For Mari, the only way she is able to balance being a successful entrepreneur and a successful mother is by setting up a strict schedule and making sure everyone at her company is aware of it. Mari always spends Mondays with her son and refuses to allow any interruptions or phone calls during the day. She and her husband also split their responsibilities with Mari being responsible for her son's morning routine before school and her husband taking care of the evenings. "Communication is key for us to make this all run as smoothly as possible," Mari says. "We have the same calendar online and we text one another during the day to make sure we're on the same page."

Mari says that their main focus always is making sure that their son is being well taken care of and that one or both parents are available to make sure his needs are being met. "I think one of the great things our son is learning is the value of entrepreneurship," Mari adds. "All these life skills, like being flexible and working hard, he's learning as he watches the business develop, and he's putting that same stuff to work in his life with his friends and with school. It's really amazing to watch as he grows older."

Because time is so critical to Mari, she also has gone to extreme lengths to make sure that her business processes are as streamlined as possible. "It's often said that you can either work in your business or on your business and I wanted to be working on it." That meant that Mari looked at every aspect of Foiled Cupcakes and has made it as streamlined as possible without compromising the cupcakes or the customer experience. "We run as efficiently as possible," Mari says proudly. "For example, we don't use piping tips in our piping bags when we put frosting on the cupcakes because that would be one more piece we would need to clean and store." Mari's goal is to cut all the fat and extras that often get layered on top of a business – specifically in handcrafted food businesses – because that just means there is more for her to manage. As an example, the Quippies, in addition to being a novel way to differentiate Foiled Cupcakes from competitors, also enables the staff to quickly and easily create branded cupcakes for corporate clients without requiring one or more staff members to pipe intricate logo designs onto each cupcake. "We can still have a great company without all that stuff – we just have to be creative in our thinking."

Mari's strategic approach to her business has helped Foiled Cupcakes become one of the leading cupcake delivery services in Chicago with clients that include Fortune 500 companies. To others thinking of starting a food business, Mari acknowledges that passion for the product is important, but so too is passion for the business. "You have to have a firm understanding of the business and if you don't, then find someone who does," Mari suggests. "I feel like it's hard to do both the business and the baking successfully and I think one of the reasons we've been successful is that my love for baking doesn't overwhelm my business sense. Like all things in life, it's about balance!"

www.foiledcupcakes.com

Do Things Differently: Following the herd just makes you one of the crowd. Mari's company gets noticed because she identified a problem – not being able to get cupcakes delivered to the suburbs – and then created her company with an eye towards solving that problem. That meant forgoing a bricks-and-mortar location like every other cupcake store in the area to keep her overhead low and her cupcakes, with delivery costs, priced in line with other cupcake stores.

Spend Money To Develop A Strong Brand. If you don't have experience in branding or graphic design, it is well worth the expense to hire a team of experts to work closely with you to develop a brand that will resonate with customers. Remember that the brand you go out to market with will be the first thing people see and experience about your company. You want to ensure it conveys the type of brand personality you want associated with your company.

Don't Be Afraid To Hire Employees. By hiring people who have strengths in areas where Mari is lacking, she has more time to work on the marketing and community-building aspect that comes so naturally to her. Mari specifically looked to hire people with strong culinary backgrounds who could focus on the baking side of the company, and Mari spends the majority of her time working to build relationships and generate sales. Don't let a lack of a culinary background stop you from starting an artisan food business. If you're passionate about the product, look to partner with or hire people who can help you with the production while you manage other aspects of the business, or vice versa.

Social Media Marketing Is Not About Sales. Done right, social media marketing can help generate sales, but those sales won't happen until after you've developed relationships online. Mari devotes a significant amount of her time to cultivating friendships via Twitter by talking about things she is passionate about. Her genuine approach to relationship-building, as opposed to using Twitter as a megaphone to push the Foiled Cupcakes name, has helped turn her Twitter fans not only into customers but also into advocates for her company.

Strive For Balance. Running your own small food business can be all-consuming if you let it. Mari creates a sense of balance both at work and in her personal life by setting boundaries. Even if you don't have employees who can manage the business on a day-to-day basis, setting "office hours" and outlining when you're willing to answer phone calls and e-mails will help create some semblance of balance in your life. While it may not always feel that way, setting aside a few hours every day for yourself and your family will ultimately make you happier – and make you a better entrepreneur.

PIG OF THE MONTH
OVERCOMING ROAD BLOCKS

When Lea Richards landed her dream job as an analyst for a large financial company she believed it was the first step in what promised to be a meteoric rise up the career ladder – and toward a New York City Wall Street lifestyle. So why did she feel so miserable?

It's no secret that the life of a first-year financial analyst is a lot of spreadsheets, number crunching, and hard work. But Lea was prepared for the 100-hour work weeks. The daughter of an entrepreneur, she had seen her father work hard to build his business and he had passed that strong Midwest work ethic along to her. Despite all that, something just wasn't right. Lea struggled to get through every day. "I was dead, drained, and constantly sick," Lea, a thin wisp of a woman, remembers. "I was asking myself whether the paycheck was worth the life I was living." Just when Lea felt like she may drown, a lifeline came in the form of a buyout offer when the firm downsized. "I took the buyout," she says, "and headed home."

Dayton, Ohio is about as far from the never-ending energy hub of New York City as you can get. Lea knew that some time at home with her family would help her figure her life out. "My dad kept telling me I should open my own business because that's the only way to make money and do what you want," Lea recalls, "but I didn't know what type of business I wanted to start." Lea tossed around ideas for months but nothing seemed just right. Either the idea wasn't feasible, there was too much competition, or it just didn't excite her.

It should be noted that Lea's family are unabashed barbecue fanatics. They have turned essentially every family vacation into a hunt for the perfect barbecue and aren't afraid to stop by an unknown hole-in-the-wall joint in their quest to find the best. One day, while Lea was ruminating on what she should do with her life, her father ordered some ribs from a well-known gourmet barbecue mail order store as a treat for the family. Sadly, the ribs did not live up to the company's marketing hype and were a disappointment to everyone. But they provided something else – an idea that could stick. "This is what you should do," Lea's father told her.

As soon as her father mentioned it, the idea appealed to Lea. Her passion for barbecue is undeniable and she'd spent years honing her grilling techniques and recipes during countless cookouts and gatherings for friends and family. Because barbeque flavors are so regional, Lea also had spent considerable time experimenting with ingredients, drawing inspiration from all her family's visits. In fact, it was a family trip to Key West, known for their famous key limes and other citrus fruits, which inspired Lea's one-of-a-kind Key West BBQ sauce that everyone always raved about.

The more Lea thought about it the more she realized that there was a market for mail-order barbecue. "No matter how accomplished a home cook is," she explains, "Barbecue ribs and other meats are usually something a home cook doesn't feel comfortable working with due to the amount of time and equipment needed for authentic barbecue. It's often just easier for the home cook to get their barbecue from someone else." In most mail-order barbeque cases, all a home cook needs to do is reheat the meat in the oven for 30-40 minutes because the barbecue is fully cooked and flash frozen before being shipped.

While there certainly are companies that ship their products, the vast majority of barbecue companies focus on selling locally, so she felt that there was room for a newcomer in the niche world of mail-order barbecue.

As the idea began to take shape in her mind, Lea started looking into what she needed to get her business up and running. Even though she didn't write a formal business plan before she started, it was important to Lea that her company use only humane meats. "I feel that it's very important to eat real whole foods," Lea says, "and not something that's filled with hormones. I think we as a country need to get away from all the additives and preservatives in our food, which I believe are causing a lot of our health problems. So I couldn't justify buying lower quality meat simply because it's cheaper."

Buying local also is equally important to Lea. She remembers her grandfather always telling her that the best way to stimulate the economy is to buy from the locally-owned store down the street. She followed that sage advice and started looking for humanely-raised meats from local producers. "It was actually relatively easy to find," Lea, who had expected it to take weeks, if not months, to source her ingredients, says. "I just asked around and talked to butchers. Once people realized I wanted to work with local producers they were more than happy to point me in the right direction." In addition to her meats, Lea also gets as many of her other ingredients from local businesses as possible; she works with a local Ohio company that specializes in spices for her spice rub combinations and contracts with a local dairy whenever she needs milk for a recipe.

Another important aspect of the business that Lea knew from Day 1 was to make sure that all her meats and sauces were made in-house. Lea wanted to keep a close eye on the quality of her products so she could personally vouch for everything that shipped to customers. To keep costs as low as possible, Lea's father helped her turn part of a commercial building he owned into a workspace and he even fabricated a 20-foot smoker for her.

With those big pieces of the business in place, you would think the rest would be easy. But getting to the point where Lea could actually sell her barbecue online took several more months. "I simply had no idea the amount of work I'd have to do with the USDA (United States Department of Agriculture)," Lea says. "When I first had the idea for Pig

Of The Month I didn't even know that I'd be regulated by the USDA, and they really put you through the wringer. It's all for a good reason, of course – to make sure that your meats are properly cooked – but I had to write a complete safety plan, I had to keep logs, I had to work with them to ensure they could be on site while we were cooking so they could oversee our procedures. The entire process took six months!"

Lea acknowledges that small food business owners who work with meat-based products and need to be overseen by the USDA require a healthy dose of patience and a willingness to work through any hurdles they encounter. The USDA, she explains, is set up to deal with large companies that are processing hundreds of thousands of pounds of meat a day and have a staff of safety officials to oversee every rule and regulation. The agency simply isn't used to working with small independently-owned artisan food companies and it sometimes can be a struggle to work through the process with them.

Lea didn't let those extra months go to waste awaiting USDA approval and instead got right to work on her marketing strategy. First and foremost, she knew she wanted to develop a brand behind the name "Pig Of The Month" that was happy and fun. "You can't eat barbecue and not be happy," she says. It should come as no surprise that someone like Lea, who drives a lime green truck, also would want a logo that's bright and colorful, too. With an eye, as always, on keeping costs low, Lea hired a graphic designer from eLance.com to help develop what Lea believes is a fun and vibrant logo that captures the heart and soul of her company.

Lea was careful to budget for a professional public relations team too. "There is this large misconception that when you put a website on the Internet it will automatically start generating sales. The truth of the matter is that it takes many months to get clients." Lea says that when it comes to meat products it can take even longer to build a client base. "It's hard for them to buy meat from someone they don't know or trust.

PR helps us build that trust and name recognition with people." So far, with the help of the PR team, Lea and Pig Of The Month have been featured on major consumer websites and highlighted by well-respected bloggers which helps bring in more and more sales every day.

While the PR team focuses on getting the big name publications and bloggers, Lea works closely with local newspapers, and the company sponsors a grilling show on the local news channel. In addition to providing the local Dayton community with helpful grilling tips and tricks, this also helps build the company's name recognition locally. This is important because local customers now can pick up their favorite Pig Of The Month order at Lea's facility.

The local business strategy was not part of Lea's original business plan, but when her internet sales business was held up by USDA red tape, Lea knew she needed to find an additional revenue stream to help fund the business. The ability to move and react quickly, Lea believes, is one of the most powerful tools an artisan food company has. While waiting on the USDA, Lea applied for and received her local health permit. That enabled Lea to start marketing Pig Of The Month as a catering company, which helped provide an initial revenue stream. Even though Pig Of The Month has a USDA license now and the online sales component of the business is growing, Lea says the catering revenue stream helps to fund the company's growth, so she plans to continue offering this service.

Ironically, Lea still finds herself working 100-hour weeks. The difference is she now loves what she's doing. "This business is my baby," she says. "I realize that no one will ever care about the business as I do. To other people this is just a job." Even though Lea does have a small and committed staff helping her, it's not uncommon for her to be hard at work packaging orders late into the night. All the hard work and long hours are worth it, she says. "I love seeing good reviews and seeing the sales grow. It always feels like you're on the brink of something big, and that's exciting and invigorating. When I look back I remember how scared I was when I first left my job and it felt like nothing was clicking and nothing was working out. But you just have to believe that if you keep working hard it will all one day work out, because it does."

Solve A Problem. Your company will more quickly gain customers if it solves a problem for them. In Lea's case, Pig Of The Month gives home cooks the ability to easily create mouth-watering barbecue. Being able to identify what problem your product solves will help you hone in on your target market. In turn, you can craft marketing messages and advertising campaigns that will appeal to them and make them more willing to purchase from you.

Build Trust. Lea recognizes that people aren't likely to purchase from a small online store if they don't recognize the name, because no trust has been built between the company and the customer. Her marketing efforts revolve around trying to build that sense of trust via local television appearances and a nationwide PR effort. Ask yourself why customers should trust you and your product and how you are going to effectively convey your trustworthiness to them.

Focus On Quality Ingredients. At its most fundamental, the key to running a successful artisan food business is to have fantastic food. Many times that is a direct result of the ingredients used in the product itself. With food costs rising, it is tempting for small food business owners to switch to lower quality ingredients to cut expenses. This could ultimately be foolish if saving a few dollars impacts the flavor or consistency of your product. Lea puts time and resources towards getting customers to come to her site and order. If she were to ship out a product made from a lower quality cut of meat, her customers may never reorder or share her company's name with friends. By spending more on good ingredients your product will speak for itself and that's the most powerful marketing you can do.

Be Patient With Rules. Life isn't fair, or so the saying goes, and that holds true for many food entrepreneurs who struggle to wade through government food mandates that weren't drafted with the artisan food entrepreneur in mind. Having a healthy dose of patience when dealing with large bureaucratic organizations will go a long way in helping you keep moving forward. As Lea points out, she understands why the USDA so heavily regulates meat products, so she does everything she can to work with the USDA inspectors to make sure her products meet or exceed their standards. While this has required significantly more record-keeping than she ever anticipated, Lea never lost faith in her idea and worked diligently to get her products licensed.

Move and React Quickly. Being able to quickly change course when needed is one of the biggest benefits of being a small business. When Lea's licenses were held up by the USDA she was able to quickly shift gears and start a local barbecue catering business to support her company while she awaited her permits. While the catering business was not originally part of her business strategy, it has provided Lea with a strong revenue stream. Having a plan in place is a great first step to getting your business going but don't be afraid to make changes to that plan if you're faced with challenges you didn't anticipate.

BAKERY

a new way to snack

GLUTEN FREE - HANDCRAFTED - VEGAN

It's often said that family and business aren't a good mix. Imagine if something goes wrong with the business or one partner fails to complete a task up to the demands of another. You still have to sit across the table from them at Thanksgiving and ask them to pass the cranberries. For Lori and Michelle Corso, that rule doesn't apply; they never considered not going into business together.

In fact, starting a business was something they talked about together frequently while growing up; they just didn't know what type of company they wanted to start. The two sisters both studied business in college and also worked part time during those four years for a start-up entrepreneur as his first two employees. "That experience really helped us see what he did behind the scenes and how he went out and marketed his company," Lori says. "It was a great learning opportunity for both of us." After they graduated, the two sisters went their separate ways; Lori to a sales role and Michelle to a retail position. They still knew they wanted to start a business and hoped to do it together. The question remained, what type of business?

Lori and Michelle are not only sisters, but also twins. So it wasn't totally surprising that when one started having health issues that were later traced to gluten, the other had the exact same problems. During the two years they worked apart from one another in corporate roles, each twin spent countless hours researching and experimenting with dishes to find meals that were tasty and wouldn't upset their digestive systems. Lori says that they both noticed a dramatic improvement in their health once they cut gluten out of their diet, so in their spare time they played with recipes to try and make their favorite baked goods gluten free.

At that time there were few gluten-free baked goods available in the Raleigh, North Carolina area, so after lots of experimentation Lori and Michelle decided that their perfect joint venture would be Twin Cakes Bakery. They started simply by bringing their goodies to several local farmers' markets to see how the public would respond. "We figured we'd give it a shot and see what happened," Lori remembers thinking.

One distinct advantage that Lori and Michelle had when starting Twin Cakes Bakery is that North Carolina has a Cottage Food Law on the books which allows food producers who make things like baked goods and jams to work out of a home kitchen. This dramatically lowered Lori and Michelle's starting costs and allowed them to test out their idea at farmers' markets with minimal financial risk. (Many other states have similar laws in place or Cottage Food Laws pending in legislation. More information about this can be found at www.smallfoodbiz.com.)

Lori says that from their very first farmers' market Twin Cakes Bakery has been a hit. Customers loved their products and many people commented that they also had been searching for gluten-free products to help improve their own health and digestion. In addition to requests for specific gluten-free items, customers also started asking the twins whether they could make any vegan options and raw food snacks.

Because vegan food products don't contain any animal-based ingredients like eggs or milk, they can and often are baked or cooked at high temperatures. This is different from raw foods which are made from wholesome ingredients that come from the earth like nuts, vegetables, and seeds, and are dehydrated at a low temperature so that the enzymes and minerals naturally found in those ingredients are kept alive. Raw foods are typically dehydrated at a temperature hovering between 105 – 118 degrees, whereas most baked goods use a temperature of 300 – 350 degrees which, some argue, can kill off the living enzymes in the products.

As more and more customers at the farmers' market started asking about raw food options, Lori and Michelle became more intrigued. When they weren't baking in their kitchen for their farmers' markets, they read everything they could about raw foods. They scoured countless blogs and books and tried to meet with anyone -- a chef or simply a local resident who had incorporated this type of diet into their lifestyle -- to educate themselves about the health benefits associated with raw foods. Michelle even went to an intensive multi-week raw food culinary course at 105 Degrees, the first raw food culinary institute in the country with a course syllabus created by famed celebrity raw foods chef Matthew Kenney.

Initially, they tested the raw food recipes themselves. As they created recipes and incorporated more and more raw foods into their diet, both Lori and Michelle noticed that their health was improving even more than it had on a gluten-free diet. Seemingly overnight, both women noticed their acne had cleared up, their hair became shinier, and they felt like their energy levels increased dramatically.

And they certainly needed that extra energy, because they started to add raw food items to their farmers' market offerings in addition to their other baked goods; splitting the table between gluten-free and raw foods. While those customers who were already familiar with raw foods jumped on the opportunity to purchase the twins' snack food items like crackers, flatbreads, and biscotti, Lori and Michelle found that those unfamiliar to raw foods were a little more hesitant to give the new items a try. "Raw foods can seem scary to some people," Lori acknowledges, "and we realized that we had to provide them with more education about what exactly raw food is."

They tried to take some of the scary out by taking the time at the markets to explain the benefits of raw foods one-on-one with customers. Lori and Michelle also started adding more information about raw foods to their Twin Cakes Bakery blog; a site they'd started and kept updated since their very first farmers' market. The blog to them is a way to connect with other people who are struggling with digestion issues or who are considering incorporating gluten-free or raw foods into their diets. "The blog is not just to promote our company," Lori explains, "but also to share recipes and experiences with other people who are suffering. Making connections with people regardless of whether or not they are our customers is very important to us. We've had people from all over the world contact us because they found us through the blog. And actually, some of the blog readers have turned into customers and have now turned into great friends."

Lori and Michelle also realized early on that they'd never convert any raw foods skeptics unless their products tasted as good – if not better – than the mass-manufactured processed food most people are used to eating. "We gave away lots of samples at the market," Lori says. She explains that whenever customers can taste their products and learns about the associated health benefits it almost always results in a sale.

Lori and Michelle so enjoyed the interactions they had with customers at farmers' markets that they never really thought about trying to sell their products wholesale to health food stores. However, customers wanted access to their products regardless of whether or not a farmers' market was taking place, so Lori and Michelle started to research selling wholesale into retail stores.

First and foremost, Lori and Michelle realized that the raw food products, with their longer shelf life due to the fact that all moisture has been dehydrated from the ingredients, would do much better at stores than the gluten-free baked items which have a significantly shorter shelf life. The twins then fine-turned their existing raw foods recipes and experimented with new items to add to their product portfolio. They also realized that they needed attractive packaging to help catch the eye of store customers. Keeping with the all-in-the-family theme, they hired their older sister, a graphic artist, to design new Twin Cakes

Bakery packaging and create stand-out marketing brochures the twins could take with them on sales calls to stores.

Unsure how the retail stores would react to their products, Lori and Michelle decided to start small. Lori remembers that they tentatively approached a local health food store first and left product information and samples for the store's buyer. "And they liked it! When we got that first wholesale account I think we were both squealing with joy. Just walking into the store and seeing our product on the shelf and getting e-mails from customers saying that they just love it. It's been so rewarding, and that's why we keep doing what we're doing," Lori explains. She and Michelle have since reached out to other health foods stores around the country with similar success.

Getting into multiple retail locations also has been a good learning experience for both Lori and Michelle as the business has grown. "As we've added to our list of wholesale clients we've been able to see what our capacity is for growth and where we can go. Do we need to purchase a new dehydrator? Do we need to move into a larger space altogether? These are things we're working through because we would definitely like to be in the big stores." Lori says.

As much as they enjoy seeing their product on stores shelves, Lori is the first to admit that the actual sales side of the business is not a strength she or her sister have. "We love making the product, but when it comes to making sales calls we have a hard time doing that because we're both very shy so going out there and talking about our product is hard for us."

Lori and Michelle have tried to overcome their discomfort with sales by setting weekly goals that outline how many stores each will contact, how many samples they will send out, and how many follow-up calls they'll make. Then, they literally schedule time into their calendar to do those things, otherwise they've found it's too easy to push off their sales responsibilities and work on something else instead. As they start to look into going after larger wholesale accounts, they also are contemplating bringing a sales professional onto the staff whose whole focus would be to get new accounts, leaving Lori and Michelle more time to be in the kitchen creating and working on new flavors.

"Bringing on people will probably be our next biggest challenge," Lori candidly explains. "It's hard, though, to bring in someone from the outside. In the past anyone we've worked with has been family members so they are as committed to the core value of the company as my sister and I are. I know a lot of entrepreneurs feel that same pressure of making sure they hire the right people to take over parts of the company and I know that it's going to be a big challenge for us."

In the meantime, the twins continue to do it all themselves. "Overall, I couldn't imagine doing this without my twin sister," Lori says. "I know that if she's here making crackers that she'll being doing the same job I'd be doing. Especially for a small business who wants to compete with the big guys, you have to have a team you trust to get you there and I, obviously, trust my sister implicitly. It's been very beneficial to have someone help me through this process and me to help her as well. It's definitely made us a stronger team and a stronger company because of it."

www.twincakesbakery.com

TWIN CAKES BAKERY
RECIPE FOR SUCCESS

Share Your Knowledge. In some form or another, every artisan food business should be willing to educate their customers. Lori and Michelle's challenge is to convince people that raw foods are not only delicious but also have a host of health benefits. Today's consumers are savvy and many want to know more about what they're eating. This means you need to make yourself an expert on the product you're selling. Making yourself an expert and sharing your information with consumers via in-person meetings, online, or on your packaging, will help build trust and convert new users.

Not All Social Media Channels Will Work. Lori and Michelle mainly use the Twin Cakes Bakery blog to share information about their company and raw foods in general. Their choice to use a blog to share this information is due in part to the fact that much of what they write about can't easily be conveyed within the character limits of some social media outlets. With all the hype surrounding the ease and accessibility of social media, artisan food entrepreneurs still need to determine which channels suit their needs and their customers' needs best. As an entrepreneur, your time is limited, so spend your time and energy using those channels that will help you reach your goals and don't feel as though you must use them all, especially if they aren't useful to you.

Think Strategically About How You'll Grow. Its fun to daydream that one day your products will line store shelves around the country, but the reality is that getting to that point takes a lot of strategy. Retailers aren't going to order from you again and again if you can't fill their orders in a timely manner, so you have to make sure your growth plans for any given year take into account how much you can actually produce. Lori and Michelle have purposefully kept their wholesale business limited to smaller stores as they determine how they can increase their production to meet the growing demand. This includes making plans for future capital expenditures for things like more equipment to help increase that production. A well-thought-out plan of how you'll meet production demands in the future should be a key piece of your growth strategy.

Identify Your Weaknesses. It sounds like a dreaded job interview question, but knowing your weaknesses as a business leader enables you to more effectively manage and build your business. Just because as an entrepreneur you have to wear many hats doesn't mean you will necessarily be good in all roles. Lori clearly points out that the sales side of the business, which is a critical component to any small food business, does not come naturally to either her or her sister. This enabled them to put procedures in place that help ensure that those sales calls get aren't pushed to the backburner. Identifying weaknesses also will help clarify what attributes you would want in any future employees. As the saying goes, the quickest way to success is to surround yourself with people who are smarter than you.

Recognize The Wholesale Difference. Going from selling directly to customers to selling wholesale to stores requires planning. As Lori and Michelle did, you will want to determine what type of shelf life your products have, whether the packaging you use is the best suited for wholesale sales (including how it looks on the shelf and whether it helps keep the products fresh), and what type of health and ingredient information the stores themselves are going to want to share with their employees. Spend time walking through the stores you want to target and see what jumps off the shelf at you, and then ask yourself why you're compelled to pick up that specific product over another. At the end of the day, retailers are more likely to bring you in and keep reordering if your product quickly moves off the shelf. You need to do all the research you can to make sure that happens.

Like thousands of people in the World Trade Center on September 11 2001, Jennie Broderick's life has changed forever. At the time, Jennie was working for a large technical data mining company as their tradeshow coordinator. Jennie remembers that she loved working for a big company and loved the beautiful office space she worked in. "I'm not super techie so I didn't love the industry," Jennie says, "but I did enjoy going to work every day." Entrepreneurship, Jennie admits, was the furthest thing from her mind.

When the planes hit the World Trade Towers that morning, that world Jennie loved so much was shattered. "We lost our office," Jennie, who is still understandably emotional when talking about the day, remembers. "It was an incredibly hectic time," she says with her voice quivering.

Despite the complete loss of their office space, the company Jennie worked for was able to get back on its feet in a new location within three days. The psychological and emotional scars ran much deeper though, and Jennie was turned off by how quickly business as usual resumed. For the next two months Jennie searched for another job, but the job market in New York City had all but dried up as the city focused on healing itself.

Jennie, who is at her core an upbeat and optimistic person, didn't let that stand in her way and decided the timing was perfect to return to school and finish her bachelor's degree. Years earlier she had enrolled in college but returned home before graduating to help her parents run their business. Now, with renewed emphasis and energy, Jennie set about earning her degree with a focus in marketing.

Unbelievably, just a year and a half later, Jennie's world was once again turned upside down. In the middle of the night a pipe burst in the Jersey City apartment she shared with her husband and the injuries the two of them sustained were so extensive that they had to be hospitalized for several months and it took them almost three years to fully recover.

During her recovery Jennie remembers taking stock of her life. "I realized that this was a great opportunity to do what I wanted with my life." While learning how to walk again and other everyday tasks most of us take for granted, Jennie spent hours thinking about what exactly it was she wanted to do with her life.

When you spend close to two years thinking about your future, you're bound to come up with a lot of ideas. Time and time again though, Jennie came back to the fact that, as simple as it sounded, baking cookies made her happy. "I grew up always baking with my mother, grandmother, and bube," Jennie says, using the Yiddish term for her other grandmother. "I also did a ton of baking while I was recovering and experimented with recipes."

Still, Jennie was hesitant to start a baked goods business. "I never saw myself as the owner of a company," she says. "My role had always been on the support level and not in a manager or director position, so I was scared." Her own worst enemy, Jennie clearly remembers thinking that she wasn't someone who could be an entrepreneur.

After much internal back and forth, she finally decided that she really had nothing to lose. Jennie didn't want to risk a large sum of money on this business venture so she decided to keep the business small to keep a cap on the expenses. Jennie filed her business licenses and started Sassy Sweet Treats with a focus on the handmade cookies and brownies that had always brought her joy. "I called it my hobby business," Jennie says, "and started it out super small by just getting a booth at a few farmers' markets. It was slow, but was perfect for what I wanted at the time."

Even though Jennie planned to keep the business small, she didn't want to skimp on branding. "Coming from a marketing background, I realized that in the beginning branding and packaging were what would set me apart from my competition," she says. "I went around to lots of farmers' markets before I started and saw that many vendors had food that was exposed and not covered. As a food business you're not supposed to have that." Instead, Jennie wanted packaging that would highlight her products, help retain freshness, and be eco-friendly too. Finding that took a lot of time and numerous trial runs, she remembers.

At first she bought expensive packaging that enhanced her brand but was, ultimately, too costly for the customer and compressed Jennie's margins significantly. That sent her back to the drawing board and she spent hours online looking at cellophane bags, silver tins, and ribbon options and walking through stores to see what types of packaging other products used. "I knew in my head what I wanted the packaging to look like and the customer experience to be," Jennie recalls, which is why she ultimately settled on resealable product bags and, for gifts or orders that need to be shipped, a metal tin tied with a ribbon. "People get the tin and it's like a metal present and they're so excited to open the gorgeous packaging to see what's inside."

Since packaging can be a large expense for a small business, for her first few years Jennie only offered customers two ribbon choices to minimize the amount of packaging inventory she'd have to buy and keep on hand. "Even at Christmas, you were either getting a pink or brown ribbon wrapped tin," she says with a laugh, and it's only been recently that she now offers customers several other ribbon colors to choose from.

In 2008, after two years of farmers' market success with Jennie constantly fielding questions from people wanting to send their out-of-town friends and family some Sassy Sweet Treats, Jennie took a break from the markets to focus on creating an online commerce portal on her website. The idea behind this web store was that it would help fulfill that desire for her treats from people who couldn't make it to the local farmers' markets and it would help Jennie build a more continuous revenue stream that wasn't so heavily dependent on the seasonal summer farmers' markets. While the site has expanded her revenue stream, Jennie says that her website also is very seasonal and receives most orders around the holidays. "One of my biggest struggles is driving traffic there year-round."

When Jennie first started thinking about building the online component to Sassy Sweet Treats, one of her major concerns was how her treats would stand up during shipment and how that might detract from the customer experience. With farmers' markets Jennie could control that experience by making a customer visit to her booth as pleasant as possible. Shipping, however, meant putting that experience in the hands of the shipping company and Jennie worried how that might impact her treats and her customers' perception of her company. In an effort to minimize the risk associated with shipping her products, Jennie did numerous test shipments to friends around the country and then asked for their candid feedback. "My friends loved this stage of the business because they'd get free treats from me," Jennie says. In exchange for the free treats though, Jennie would ask her friends to take pictures when the package arrived and give her a detailed account of how the products had fared during transit. "You will never receive a dented tin from me," Jennie says proudly, "because my quality control standards are too strict. I have an image my business must uphold and a dent will detract from that image."

After a year off from the farmers' markets to get the new site up and running, Jennie decided to return to the markets and merge it with her growing online business. Unfortunately, she found that in her absence new competitors had moved into her space. As Jennie explains, farmers' markets in her area don't like to have too many of the same kind of vendors and Jennie was locked out of many of her old markets. She was finally accepted into a handful of markets and, while on the waiting list for others, takes her business to festivals and focuses on catering to fill the gap. "I regret that I left my markets," Jennie says candidly, "but I firmly believe that everything happens for a reason."

Like many artisan food entrepreneurs, Jennie knows that she needs to advertise to help drive web traffic, but she's hesitant to spend the money. "I don't want to spend money unless I absolutely have to and if I do, I want to see results," she says. Since results can be hard to gauge in advertising, for now Jennie relies on social media as the mainstay of her marketing strategy. To engage fans on Facebook, she puts up questions and offers free cookies to people who post on her page. "I don't want it to just be me on Facebook because that's not interesting," she explains, "so I try to make it an interactive experience."

Even though Twitter is a core piece of most small business' social media plans, Jennie was slow to embrace it, but now finds Twitter invaluable to her success. "I used to send out an e-newsletter but it was packed with so much information that I lost people part way through," Jennie explains. "Twitter is another way I can share that information and interact with a community." Because an entrepreneur's life can be so busy, she specifically sets aside time every day to check in on Twitter. "I try to check in every four hours," she says. "There are a lot of small businesses out there that think they don't have the time for social networking sites, but it really takes limited time and can be some of the cheapest marketing you ever do." To facilitate all of this, Jennie upgraded to a smartphone, which lets her access Facebook and Twitter from anywhere. Calling it one of the best decisions she's made, the smartphone enables her to check in regardless of whether she's in the kitchen baking or standing in line at the post office waiting to ship an order.

The saying goes that entrepreneurs must be willing to wear many hats and Jennie is no different. She runs every aspect of Sassy Sweet Treats, from the baking to the banking, though her business has grown so much that she sometimes has to coerce her husband into helping her package treats at night. "I'm at the point where I need help, but I'm afraid to give up control," she says. Jennie also admits that the idea of managing other people scares her. She's not the type to tell other people what to do, so she has been practicing her management skills on her husband.

"When I first taught my husband how to package, his results weren't perfect. So I sat down with him and explained how the package should look and why that is important to the brand. Then I leaned back and asked him how I came across. I want his feedback because I want to be a good boss. To me, that means being able to address problems in a respectful manner because then employees will respect your business."

Jennie credits her husband, along with the rest of her friends and family as being her rock throughout her business' growth. However, she does warn other artisan food entrepreneurs that everyone, even strangers, also will have ideas for how you should run your business. When someone approaches her with an idea, which happens more frequently than most people's patience would allow, Jennie says she's learned to listen, smile, and then continues on the path that is true to herself and her business goals. "I trust my instincts now and I believe that's important in business," she says.

That trust wasn't always there as Jennie remembers back to her life before Sassy Sweet Treats. "I never thought I was going to be my own boss," she says, "but that was just me getting in my own way and holding myself back. I think everyone is capable of doing this, but a lot of people hold themselves back. I'm doing something I didn't think I was capable of and I love it."

Bigger Is Not Necessarily Better. Starting small, by just focusing on a handful of farmers' markets, is an excellent and low-cost way to test your business concept with the public. It enables you to see if there is demand for your products, allows you to play with price points to determine what will work best, and it gives you a chance to find out whether running this business on a day-to-day basis is something you really want to do. While Jennie was in the position to devote most of her time to her new business, starting small also is a great way for anyone working full-time at another job to test the waters without giving up the financial security and benefits of their other job.

Packaging Is Part Of The Experience. Jennie recognized from the beginning that her packaging would say as much, if not more, about her products and her company as the products themselves. If your product needs packaging, you cannot underestimate how important appearance is to customers when making a buying decision. When determining what type of packaging you want for your products, look at it from the customers' point of view and ask how they will likely use your goods. Jennie realized that most people won't eat all the cookies or brownies in her package at once, so she puts her products in resealable bags. This keeps Jennie's cookies and brownies fresh from first bite to last.

Customers Are Key – Even If They're 800 Miles Away. The fact that Jennie tested shipments of her products across the country prior to setting up an online store shows how much she values her customers. Having one of her orders arrive dented takes away from the experience Jennie wants customers to have when they receive her treats. This level of attention to detail is one of the reasons why Jennie's internet sales business continues to grow. If you ship your products to customers or retailers, make sure you've tested how well your products ship to a variety of locations and in different weather conditions. Do you

. to ship your product with ice in the hot summer months? If your
. der is held up for three days due to a snow storm will the product still
be as good as if it were delivered on time? Developing contingency
plans will help you cope when shipments are damaged, missed, or late,
and working with affected customers to quickly remedy the situation
will go a long way in helping you build a business people view as
trustworthy and reliable.

Selectively Listen. It can be exhausting to constantly field advice
on how to improve your business, but remember that in most
cases those who are commenting only want to help you succeed. While
it's always important to listen to customer feedback, don't be too quick
to follow every suggestion. Of course, as a savvy businessperson you
already know that trying to contradict these people would not be a wise
use of your time or energy, nor would it necessarily endear you or your
company to them. In that case Jennie's approach is best – simply smile,
nod, and say that you'll take their ideas under consideration.

Get Out Of Your Own Way. Jennie said it best when she
mentioned that the biggest hurdle she had to overcome in
starting her business was simply getting out of her own way. Many
people are their own worst enemy and don't believe they have the skills
or ability to start a successful artisan food business. Remember, starting
and running an artisan food business is not brain surgery. Your job is to
create delicious food that makes people happy – how hard can that be?
Trust in yourself and make your dreams happen.

GALLOLEA ORGANICS
LISTENING TO CUSTOMERS

Tom Gallo's grandmother was understandably proud of her handmade tomato sauce. Based on a secret family recipe handed down to her, Tom's grandmother had spent hours in the kitchen refining the simmering pots of tomato sauce with her own combination of herbs. The result was a unique and complex flavor profile that made her pasta dishes the envy of the neighborhood. She never could have guessed though that one day, years later, that same tomato sauce would be what helped save her beloved grandson during the biggest economic upheaval since the Great Depression. By the same token though, Tom Gallo and his wife Susan Devitt never imagined that they would one day start an all-natural pizza kit business.

The circumstances that led this husband and wife team to start GalloLea Organics is a common story in the U.S. these days. Prior to the Great Recession, Tom had worked as a ceramics engineer. Over the years, Tom watched as more and more jobs in his highly specialized industry were outsourced to China and India. While at one point Tom and Susan, who at that time owned and ran her own graphic design business, briefly contemplated moving abroad to follow the jobs, they ultimately decided that they didn't want to leave their mountain home in Ashville, North Carolina.

Then, in 2008, the real estate bubble burst and Susan's largest client, who happened to be in the construction industry, canceled her contract. As the economy continued to slow, more and more of Susan's clients pulled back on their spending leaving Susan and Tom, who was by now officially unemployed, facing financial doom. Tom and Susan again considered moving elsewhere to find jobs, but, by then the financial meltdown had spread worldwide.

Between a rock and a hard place, Tom started to wonder whether it would be possible to sell his grandmother's tomato sauce. Tom received the recipe before his grandmother passed away and it never failed to gain rave reviews from friends. What's more, the tomato sauce recipe called for old-fashioned techniques that focused on using all-natural ingredients with no added preservatives or sugars like the commercially-manufactured sauces that line store shelves. "I started to think that this was a way we could make something that was healthier and better tasting at the same time," Tom says.

Enrolling in a food business course proved discouraging though. Tom and Susan realized that the pasta sauce market was so competitive it would be difficult for a new artisan brand to break in, even with the all-natural angle. Rather than giving up on the idea entirely, Susan and Tom brainstormed about how they could morph their original idea into another possible business venture. In one of those brainstorming sessions, Tom and Susan were discussing ways that they enjoyed using the tomato sauce and that all-American favorite, pizza, came up. As so often happens when people collaborate, Tom and Susan began to wonder if it would be possible to create a product that people could use to easily and quickly make pizza at home from scratch. "We wanted the pizzas to be fresh, homemade, and a way for family and friends to sit down and enjoy a meal together," Susan says.

Over the course of the next six months, Susan and Tom spent every spare moment experimenting with pizza dough recipes. They used feedback from friends and family to tweak their idea. They also took classes in business law, started working on their business plan, and became certified in canning – a necessary component of selling tomato sauce commercially. By 2010, their experimentations were complete, and Tom and Susan had designed a make-at-home pizza kit that included everything customers needed to make their own homemade pizza. The original pizza kits contained an all-natural whole wheat pizza dough mix that customers add water to, a pouch of Tom's grandmother's tomato sauce, and a round of parchment paper for customers to use during baking to help optimize the crust's texture. All customers have to add is their favorite toppings.

Developing a product they believed would sell was one thing, but figuring out how to wrap all these components together into one eye-catching package that would make customers want to buy it was another problem entirely. Given her graphic design background, this challenge was right up Susan's alley and she eagerly attacked it. "The company name itself is a combination of Tom's last name and our friend Lea, who has always been one of our biggest cheerleaders," says Susan, noting how she mulled over various name ideas before landing on GalloLea Organics. "Plus, I like that it's a play on the name Galileo."

Then Susan went to work designing the packaging itself. "Since the product is made from organic ingredients I wanted the packaging to have an organic feel as well," Susan says. To achieve this, she painted the logo by hand and then had a friend take a picture. That hand painting is the image that's used on all of GalloLea Organic's labels. This logo, Tom and Susan believe, helps create the natural and handmade aesthetic that differentiates their company from competitors.

Picking the product packaging was a little less straight-forward, however. Originally, GalloLea Organics' pizza kits were only available in beautiful kraft boxes that contained two kits each. While the box itself looked great on store shelves, the price point for the two kits was too high for many customers, especially those who were unfamiliar with the GalloLea Organics name and were hesitant to spend upwards of $7 for a product they hadn't tried before. Despite the fact that Susan hated to make the change, the couple ultimately decided on a package that could hold just one kit. After lots of trial and error, they switched over to natural brown bags that fit with Tom and Susan's vision for their brand. "I was very nervous to leave the box and ordered in a lot of different bag samples, but eventually I found a bag that I love and that retailers love," Susan says. Equally as important, consumers love the single-serving bag and it's become a fast seller partly, Susan acknowledges, because of the lower price point.

Finding a price point that customers are comfortable with is obviously a critical piece of any new food business, but taste and, in the case of make-at-home pizza kits, the convenience, are equally as important, too. Before Susan and Tom tried to sell their kits to retailers they gave 40 sample kits out to strangers and asked for feedback. Susan laughs when she says that the feedback they got from these strangers was more helpful than what they received from most of their friends. That type of candid feedback, which typically only strangers feel comfortable giving, helped Tom and Susan see where they needed to make changes. Overall the feedback was very positive, though, and proved to Tom and Susan that there was a market for their pizza kits.

The next big hurdle was to try and get GalloLea Organics pizza kits onto store shelves. No easy task, Susan and Tom first approached their local grocery and specialty stores. Since Ashville is a close-knit community, in most cases they were able to set up meetings with store owners and talk directly with them about their product. Most of the time, the local stores would agree to bring in GalloLea Organics on a trial basis. To truly grow though, Tom and Susan knew that they were going to have to aim at getting into one of the big natural food stores in the area. They set their sights on Earth Fare, a natural grocer with multiple stores in the Mid-Atlantic region, but calls to the grocery buyer went unanswered. Finally, sick of leaving voicemails and getting no response, Susan decided to drive to Earth Fare's corporate headquarters. She showed up at 4 p.m. and asked the receptionist if she could meet with the grocery buyer. "I was shocked when they actually let me see the grocery manager, but I showed him [our kits] and he thought it looked great," Susan remembers. "He happened to be heading into a meeting with his supervisor and wanted to take a sample with him and by the time I got home we had an e-mail complete with paperwork to see if we could fit into their stores!"

Susan says that when it comes to getting into grocery stores she now fervently believes that you have to keep asking until you finally get an answer. Nine times out of 10 they don't return phone calls or unsolicited e-mails. "You really feel like you're being a pest," Susan says, "but you have to believe in your product and just keep trying to get your company in front of them."

Tom and Susan also quickly learned that just because your product is in a store doesn't mean people will actually buy it. "We would go and look for our product in stores and we couldn't even find ourselves due to poor shelf placement," Susan says. "Half of the battle is marketing to consumers so that they know to look for your product." To achieve this on their very limited marketing budget, Tom and Susan have found that their best resource is to do in-store demonstrations. "When we do demonstrations our products sell really well," Tom says. "People definitely want to taste a new product before they buy it. The question we now face is how we can continue growing the business because we can't be in every store every weekend doing demos."

It was during these in-store demonstrations that Tom and Susan started receiving requests from shoppers for gluten-free pizza kit options. It got to the point where they were being asked about this at almost every demonstration so Tom and Susan felt compelled to listen. With what little extra time they could squeeze out of their schedules they started experimenting with gluten-free pizza dough options. Since a good friend of Tom and Susan's had been diagnosed with celiac disease, they had an expert they could turn to who was able to point them to resources about gluten-free ingredients. This friend also acted as the main taste-tester on the many versions of gluten-free dough Tom created during his practice runs.

Throughout this experimentation phase, which took several months, Tom was focused on not only making a pizza dough that met the gluten-free requirements, but one that actually tasted good, too. In their conversations with shoppers who asked for gluten-free options, they had heard numerous complaints about the lack of flavor in gluten-free products. Tom and Susan wanted their pizza dough to stand apart and live up to the standards they'd laid out for GalloLea Organics.

Their hard work has paid off and the GalloLea Organics gluten-free pizza kit has become their best-selling product. It's not uncommon for Tom and Susan to receive phone calls from gluten-free customers thanking them for helping bring pizza back into their lives. Tom and Susan also have found that because the gluten-free community is so tightly connected, thanks in part to the internet, that sales of their gluten-free kit have grown substantially with minimal marketing.

Susan seized on this opportunity and sent pizza kit samples to influential gluten-free food bloggers. Susan found that the online reviews these bloggers posted boosted sales so much that she now regularly buys banner ad space on those key sites to help promote the company. "We also spend advertising money doing Google Adwords," Susan says, explaining their advertising strategy. "Because we are able to tightly focus on the gluten-free community we can craft ads that directly target that demographic with Google."

While online ads and blog reviews certainly help drive web traffic and are a cost-effective way for Tom and Susan to share GalloLea Organics with a wider audience, they still love interacting one-on-one with customers and with one another. "Not every relationship would survive starting a business together," Susan says of her marriage and business partnership with Tom. "Someone said to us that food is communion – it brings people together and that's been true in our lives too. I don't know how people start a business by themselves. You have to be incredibly passionate about your product to make it successful in today's market and tenacious about selling it to retailers and customers. It takes a lot of time and energy and I can't imagine not having a strong partner to help you."

GALLOLEA ORGANICS
RECIPE FOR SUCCESS

Change Can Be Hard But Good. When Susan and Tom started GalloLea Organics, Susan had a very definite idea of how she wanted the product packaging to appear. Unfortunately, as she found out, that packaging made the product too expensive for their customers. While you may have an image in your head of how you want your products to look or how you want the company to grow, remain flexible. Changing course is not a sign of failure on your part, but rather is a reflection of your ability to quickly adapt to an ever-changing marketplace. Being nimble is a good thing.

Ask For Critical Feedback. The only way your company will be successful is if customers actually like what you're selling. Before you go to market, ask for critical feedback. Most entrepreneurs simply ask friends and family for their thoughts but Susan and Tom recognized the need for an unbiased response. Therefore, it can be valuable to ask strangers for their opinion on all aspects of your product from taste to packaging as they will often offer a more frank assessment. Their recommendations can be vital in helping you create a product that will be more widely accepted by the marketplace.

Be Persistent. Unless you are a born salesman, sales are hard, there's no doubt about that. It can be disheartening to send your product out to retailers and receive no reply at all regardless of how often you follow-up with phone calls or e-mails. But, as Susan showed, persistence can be rewarded. Don't let a lack of response from a buyer stand in your way. Figure out if you can set up a meeting with the buyer; if a store manager is enthusiastic about your product see if s/he might be willing to take it to the buyer; try to determine if the buyers attend area tradeshows that you might be able to participate in; or you can always take a page from Susan's playbook and show up at the corporate headquarters unannounced! You have to be your company's own best advocate, so be persistent.

Listen To What Your Customers Are Saying. While this seems counter to Sassy Sweet Treat's Recipe To Success, which suggests customer comments should be taken with a grain of salt, if you notice that a number of people are requesting similar changes to your product then it may very well be worthwhile to listen. By listening to customers, Tom and Susan were able to create a product that met the demand for gluten-free pizza kits. Because small food entrepreneurs are more likely to sell their products straight to customers or do more in-store demonstrations than the large brands, they have the opportunity to receive immediate feedback. Small food entrepreneurs can oftentimes recognize a trend and develop a product that fits that criteria before the larger brands are even aware the demand exists. Use your company's size to your advantage and listen to what customers are asking for. If you hear the same thing again and again from different people you may very well be able to tap into a demand that the larger brands can't fulfill.

Get More Bang For Your Marketing Buck. Positioning one or more products in your company's portfolio as a niche product, like Tom and Susan did with their gluten-free pizza kit, is a cost-effective way to maximize your marketing dollars. By focusing on the tight-knit gluten-free and celiac online communities, Susan has been able to get more press and blogger reviews of their gluten-free product than their original pizza kit has ever received. Susan also is able to target their marketing efforts at the gluten-free community via ads on well-respected gluten-free websites and blogs, and by using keywords in pay-per-click searches. Again, because she is targeting a smaller, more defined audience, the money she spends on marketing has a better return on investment than marketing done for the original pizza kit, which must compete in the hyper-crowded "regular pizza" market.

TROPICAL TRADERS SPECIALTY FOODS
CREATING A VISIONS-ORIENTED BUSINESS

To fully understand the story of how Rebeca Krones and Luis Zevallos started Tropical Traders Specialty Foods, a distribution company for Royal Hawaiian Honey, you have to step back a generation. It technically all started with Rebeca's father, Michael Krones, who first learned about beekeeping in the 1970s while living in Costa Rica. He quickly fell in love with the industrious creatures that not only produce honey but also are responsible for the pollination that results in an estimated one-third of all U.S. food production.

After moving to the Hawaii's Big Island, Michael started his own apiary in 1996 which he called Hawaiian Queen Co. While Michael's nearly 1,500 hives produce honey, the mainstay of his business is the exportation of queen bees. As Rebeca explains, "requeening (introducing a new queen into the hive) or having a strong queen is crucial for the hives, so most commercial beekeepers requeen every year or two. Honey is an obvious bi-product of keeping bees, so for years Rebeca's father simply collected the honey and sold it to honey packers who blended it with honey from other producers and shipped it off to supermarket shelves.

What many consumers don't know is that blended honey is a far cry from raw honey. To successfully blend honey and prevent natural crystallization from making the honey hard, many mass-manufactured honey brands heat the honey they purchase to high temperatures. This, in effect, changes the chemical composition of the honey, which enables the blending of honey from many different beekeepers. Mass-manufactured honey also is pressure-filtered which, beekeepers say, removes much of the natural health benefits of honey. Not to mention that blended honey has a uniform and, some would argue, bland taste when compared to raw honey.

Despite her family's background, Rebeca had no intention of going into her father's business. She originally had her eye on the art world and left the pristine white sand beaches and warm tropical winds of Hawaii for New York where she studied art history. While in college she had the opportunity to intern with the Metropolitan Museum of Art and, after graduation, she moved to San Francisco to work for some of the area's most prestigious art galleries.

Over time, Rebeca realized that she lacked the driving passion for art necessary for a career in that industry. "I wanted to wake up every morning excited to get started," she says, "and I realized that what I really wanted was to become an entrepreneur."

Given Rebeca's family connections in the beekeeping world, it may come as no surprise that her entrepreneurial pursuits led her back to where she started. But the truth of the matter is that Rebeca's reason for focusing on honey ran far deeper than simply having access to an apiary.

Not only is the raw honey from Rebeca's father's apiary mouthwateringly sweet, it also comes from a single-source – something few other honey brands can claim. Single-source means that in addition to being collected from one beekeeper, the honey is collected by bees that focus on one specific type of plant or flower at a time. Hawaii's Big Island has three distinct floral blooms throughout the year, so for skilled Hawaiian beekeepers it's possible to trace the honey in the hive at any given time to one of the specific blooms. Just as wine is impacted by the specific soil and weather endured by the grapes, so too is honey. A single-source honey from one bloom cycle can taste remarkably different from honey collected from those same hives at another time of the year.

And that's why Rebeca and her husband Luis created the Royal Hawaiian Honey brand, which buys all of its honey exclusively from Michael's apiary. The flavors offered by Royal Hawaiian Honey correspond to the three blooms Hawaii experiences annually. Thus, there is the Macadamia Nut Blossom honey, Lehua honey, and

Christmas Berry honey. To help with the distribution of the brand, they started Tropical Traders Specialty Foods, which is based in Oakland, California.

While Rebeca and Luis knew a lot about honey and beekeeping, they felt that they needed to know more about how to start and successfully operate a business before they invested too much time and money into the process. For that they turned to their local Small Business Administration office and made full use of the resources available to them there. "Literally, I think we took about 40 classes," Rebeca says, laughing. "We were there all the time!" Through their Small Business Administration office they got in touch with a woman whose sole focus is working with food-based businesses. She was able to help Rebeca and Luis build a business plan, clarify their goals, and now even several years later they still meet once a month to make sure the business is on track and hitting quarterly financial goals. "Most entrepreneurs will write a business plan, but they don't go back to it," Rebeca says. "We work from our budget and from our goals every day. We do a 90-day goal planning session every quarter to figure out where we're going and how we plan on getting there."

As they created their business plan, Rebeca and Luis had several conversations about what was important to them as individuals and how they wanted to incorporate those values into the business. While most small businesses focus on profit first, Rebeca and Luis wanted their business to stay true to their own personal values as well. "I think for most businesses one of the most important things you can do is figure out what your values are and everything you decide from that moment on radiates from those values," Rebeca says.

Because of Rebeca and Luis' passion for single-source raw honey, and Michael's focus on sustainable beekeeping, it should come as no surprise that one of the main values of Tropical Traders Foods and Royal Hawaiian Honey is to be as environmentally responsible as possible. It's certainly true that many companies claim to be eco-friendly, but for

Rebeca and Luis, being green is more than making a few environmentally responsible business decisions. It is the foundation by which they make every decision about the business.

It all starts with Michael's apiary, which has the distinction of being one of the few certified organic apiaries in the country. Before Michael places his hives on a new location, it's inspected by an organic certification association to ensure that the bees won't come in contact with any pesticides or other unnatural materials. This not only means keeping bees on properties that never use pesticides but that the bees must also be kept away from highways and other areas that contain a higher percentage of pollutants. Given that bees obviously fly from the hive to collect pollen, finding the perfect spot is not an easy task and Michael takes special care in choosing where his hives will go.

Rebeca and Luis wanted to carry that concern for the environment through as much of their products' lifecycle as possible and one big componant was finding environmentally-friendly packaging. They talked to other entrepreneurs and spent hours searching on their own for biodegradable shipping boxes and packaging. "We are selling a certified organic product," Rebeca says, "and we felt that if the product was going to be environmentally responsible then everything else needs to follow that same trend. Otherwise, it doesn't make sense to us."

Not all environmentally-friendly decisions are that easy, though. One of the challenges Rebeca and Luis face is the fact that the hives are located on Hawaii, which is a long way from their offices in California. "We hand-pack all of our honey ourselves in Hawaii," Rebeca says. This means that the containers, which they source through a mainland manufacturer, are shipped all the way to Hawaii first. Then the containers are filled in Hawaii and shipped thousands of miles back to California.

There have been other trade-offs, too. At first, Rebeca and Luis were packing the honey in glass containers but it wasn't at all energy efficient to ship bulky and heavy glass containers to Hawaii and then ship the even heavier honey-filled containers back to California. After many months of searching, Rebeca was able to find tapered plastic tubs that can be nested inside one another for shipping to Hawaii, which minimizes their cargo size and weight.

While the plastic tubs can be recycled, not every municipality has the ability to recycle that type of plastic. Rebeca is able to reconcile this. "Most customers only think about a product being environmentally-friendly from when they get it to throwing it away, in which case the glass containers are better since those can be recycled everywhere," she says. "But there's more happening on the manufacturing side. We determined that because we were shipping to and from the mainland, that using the plastic containers actually used less energy and were better for the environment overall."

It turns out that the plastic versus glass issue was just the beginning in a long line of decisions they've had to make about the role their company plays in the environment. "When we really started to get really, really green was when we decided to become carbon neutral," Rebeca explains. Even after they swapped the glass for the lighterweight plastic containers, Rebeca and Luis still struggled with the impact so much shipping back and forth has on the environment. For that reason they decided to get in touch with CarbonFund and see what steps they could take to become carbon neutral. CarbonFund is a third party organization that helps them calculate the carbon footprint of Royal Hawaiian Honey's operations. Rebeca and Luis then pay CarbonFund for every penny of CO_2 their operations create and that money is invested in environmentally-sensitive projects.

With the help of CarbonFund, Royal Hawaiian Honey was the first honey brand to earn the right to be called carbon neutral. As Rebeca explains, "being environmentally-responsible came from the fact that we were on farms and we can see the impact of not treating the environment well. It's been the way that we choose to live our lives.

The truth of the matter is that it can be very expensive for a small business to integrate things like biodegradable packaging and carbon offsets. Plus, while many consumers say that they want more environmentally-friendly products, Rebeca and Luis found that this doesn't automatically translate into more sales. Rebeca admits that she thought being carbon-neutral would boost sales more than it has, but now realizes that consumers don't yet fully understand the carbon-neutral concept. Rebeca and Luis learned that consumer education needs to be a big part of their marketing strategy. "The challenge as an artisan producer is explaining the value proposition to the customers," Rebeca explains. "We believe in the benefit of our honey and in what we're doing, and when we're able to educate customers about that the value becomes much more apparent to them. That's the goal, but it's difficult to position that on a larger scale when you don't have a big marketing budget."

Rebeca and Luis have had success getting their honey onto store shelves through industry tradeshows where they're able to meet, talk with, and educate retailers about the benefits of their honey. Though tradeshows can be prohibitively expensive for many artisan brands, Rebeca is quick to point out that there are resources available to small businesses if you're willing to look for them. Because their honey is produced in Hawaii, Rebeca and Luis were able to take advantage of the Western United States Agricultural Trade Association's (WUSATA) Branded Program. WUSATA is a nonprofit organization made up of 13 western states to help promote locally-made food and agricultural products by offsetting some tradeshow and marketing costs for businesses that meet their criteria.

Not surprisingly, Royal Hawaiian Honey currently sells best in Hawaii. "Customers just love the fact that it's produced and bottled here in Hawaii," Rebeca says. In fact, their honey is so popular that it was picked up by Costco's Hawaiian stores. "Building this distribution business has been a really interesting experience," Rebeca says. "There are challenges when it comes to building a food business here in the

U.S. and I've learned a tremendous amount about how food is produced, how it's distributed, and the role of retailers in all of this."

As she explains, when it comes to wholesale accounts the big conundrum is how to make your product jump off a crowded shelf and attract customers' attention. "The most difficult thing is not getting into a store, but staying there!" Rebeca says. Discounting your product's price can help, but that cuts into your margins, and buying ad space for attention-grabbing ads can cost more money than many small food businesses have. "We did a lot of in-store demonstrations when we first started," Rebeca says, "in fact we still do a lot! Once people can try the product, they can really tell the difference and that converts them."

They also rely heavily on public relations as a way to help them educate consumers to the benefits of their honey and get their brand name in front of customers. The company's website includes a tremendous amount of information about not just the honey itself but also the important role sustainable beekeeping plays in the health of the environment. To complement that, they use social media tools like Facebook and a company blog to help spread the word. It's obviously working as the company's web sales have been growing every quarter.

Though the bee hives of Hawaii may seem like a world away from New York City's famed Metropolitan Museum of Art, Rebeca argues that the two are closer then they appear. "Art and honey are both extremely creative," she says. "Being an entrepreneur, you also have to be incredibly creative and on your toes at all times. When you're presented with a challenge, you have to walk through it and figure it out."

As much as she loves being a small food business owner, Rebeca advises other aspiring food entrepreneurs to spend some time trying to figure out if their idea is feasible before jumping in with both feet. "You have to do some homework and see what the competition is like. Go to the grocery stores and see what products are on the shelves and what their prices are," she advises. "I think there's a difference between your friends and family saying they love your product and the general public loving it and being willing to buy it. If you can, find a counselor or mentor who can help you through the process. Business is not rocket science, it's usually just common sense, but it helps to have someone walk with you through the process."

TROPICAL TRADERS SPECIALTY FOODS
RECIPE FOR SUCCESS

Take Advantage Of Expert Resources. It would be impossible to know absolutely everything you need to know before starting an artisan food business. Relieve yourself of that pressure by searching out experts who can help guide you through the process. Rebeca credits her local Small Business Administration office with playing a huge role in helping her create a viable business plan for Tropical Trades Specialty Foods. Identifying classes you can take, actively seeking mentors, or creating a board of advisors, will help ensure that you have people on your side to help you succeed and who will be willing to share their knowledge and expertise.

Create A Mission To Guide You. From the very first day, Rebeca and Luis set out to create a company that was in line with their personal values. Most artisan food entrepreneurs start companies that they want to be proud of, and one large component of this can be determining what values your company will hold true to as it engages in business. Just as you spend time figuring out your business plan or marketing strategy, invest time in identifying and outlining the values you want your company to stay true to and then use those values to help you make decisions you can be proud of.

Set Goals – And Hold Yourself Accountable. It's not uncommon for a small food business owner to write a business plan and then lock it away in a drawer only to forget about it in the midst of the day-to-day craziness that comes with running a business. Rebeca and Luis use their business plan to guide their business decisions every day. In addition to laying out the goals they hope to achieve that year, they also set milestones they want to hit throughout the year. By regularly checking back with their plan and those milestones they can make sure that they are on track. Check in frequently with your plan rather than being surprised at the end of the year that you didn't make the goals you'd set out to achieve.

Seek Out Industry Organizations. Just because you're small doesn't mean you're totally alone. Rebeca and Luis have had great luck working with industry organizations, which makes things like financing expensive tradeshows a possibility even on their limited budget. Industry organizations can be a great help in that they can provide resources for education, direct you to experts who can answer industry-specific questions, or, in some cases, even provide funding. When looking for industry organizations don't limit yourself strictly to the products you produce. There may be organizations set up specifically to help small businesses of all types in your state or those that are dedicated to working with minority, veteran, or women-owned businesses.

Be A Passionate Advocate For Your Product. No one cares as much about your product as you do. To most people, honey is just honey, so it behooves Tropical Traders Specialty Foods to get consumers to think a little differently. Through their website, press releases, and interactions with retail buyers and customers, Rebeca and Luis can share what makes their product vastly different than anything else on store shelves. Because most artisan food products cost more than similar mass-manufactured products, this type of passionate information-sharing also can help convince a customer that the additional cost of your product is worth it. Perhaps it also can turn a customer into an advocate for your brand.

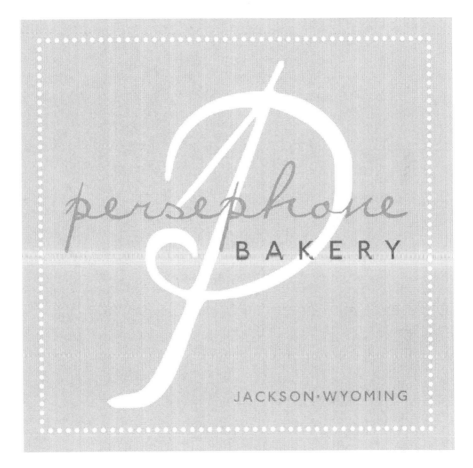

PERSEPHONE BAKERY
STEPPING AWAY BEFORE MOVING FORWARD

Jackson, Wyoming, better known to most as Jackson Hole, is home to of one of the most challenging ski mountains in the world. Travelers from all over the world come here for the fly fishing, skiing, and the proximity to Yellowstone National Park. But croissants? Kevin Cohane says yes.

Like many living in Jackson, Kevin's move from the East Coast to the mountains of Wyoming in 2003 was prompted by a simple desire to do something more with his life than spend every day sitting in a cubicle pushing paper. With the single goal of spending as much time as possible enjoying the outdoors, Kevin took a job prep cooking at a restaurant, a position that required he work mostly late afternoon and at night and left his daytime hours free to play outside.

. While working as a prep cook he had the opportunity to work a bit with bread and quickly fell in love with the hands-on techniques inherent in creating quality bread. His passion and focus were soon noticed by others and before long he was promoted up the kitchen hierarchy to a line cook position which, ironically, took him away from working with bread. "I tried to get more work in baking," Kevin recalls. "Unfortunately, there's not a lot of demand for that type of skill in this town. Most of the restaurants at the time were using frozen bread products from large wholesale suppliers."

The more time Kevin spent in Jackson the more it dawned on him that this was the perfect area to start a bakery. In addition to his own love for the area there was very limited competition for the French-inspired products he wanted to offer. Kevin believed there could be enough wholesale demand to support the business even during the slower months between the busy summer and winter tourist seasons. "I knew this would be a good area," Kevin remembers thinking, "and I was dead-set on creating this business."

Unfortunately, that meant that Kevin had to leave his beloved Jackson to fine-tune his baking skills. Kevin swapped Wyoming for the renowned culinary school in Paris, Le Cordon Bleu. There he studied the fine art of making pastries and breads. Afterward, as he says, he taste-tested his way through most of Paris before moving to Chicago, where he secured a position at the famous Fox and Obel bakery. All along, he never lost sight of his goal. "The whole time I was there I was focused on learning as much as possible," Kevin says, "so that I could come back and open up a bakery in Jackson."

Le Cordon Bleu provided Kevin with basic training in pastry, but it was at Fox and Obel where he was able to learn about the business of running a bakery. "Things like what amount of production can be done on what size equipment, what specific equipment you need, and where to get it" Kevin explains. "That kind of stuff can be a painful and expensive exercise to try and figure out on your own. Production baking is a lot different from baking bread at home, so it was also good for me to have the practical experience of working next to guys who had been doing this for decades."

Finally, in 2010, Kevin and Ali, his wife (whom he met in Jackson years earlier), decided it was time to move back to Wyoming and start building the business Kevin had been dreaming about for years. As much as they had prepared for the move though, they still faced two rather big financial hurdles. Jackson, Wyoming owes its natural beauty in part because of strict building covenants that require that 97 percent of the land in the area remain undeveloped. This, not surprisingly, has created a very high cost of living for anyone hoping to move into the area and even more so for anyone who also happens to be simultaneously looking for space to open a bakery. "The original idea was to have a wholesale and retail space in town," Kevin says, referring to the main square around which most retail businesses in the area are centered, "but it was just cost prohibitive to find a space that met our needs."

Not willing to give up on his vision entirely, Kevin altered his plan slightly and began searching for a large workspace on the outskirts of town that would enable him to build out the bakery to his specifications. While this meant he wouldn't have a retail location that people would walk by during their stroll through town, Kevin was able to find warehouse space in a price range he could afford. As a plus, the business and health permitting for that location was slightly easier than it would have been for a location in town.

Another challenge Kevin faced was getting the warehouse space built out in a manner that met Kevin's exacting standards and as well as the area health codes. Creating a bakery from scratch is a big task, and despite the easier permitting process, building the bakery took two months longer to complete than originally anticipated. Part of this was due to the amount of plumbing and electrical work the space needed so it could handle the type of equipment needed to create the authentic European flavors Kevin wanted. Compounding the problem was the fact that the nearest metropolitan area is five hours away, so most of the ovens and other pieces of specialty machinery Kevin ordered from Europe had to be trucked into the mountains. "Just getting the equipment into our space through our 12-by-12 door was tough," Kevin says, with a laugh, "I'm glad that the equipment companies took care of the logistics of actually getting the equipment up here!"

With delays eating up precious time until the summer tourist season started, Kevin began testing and tweaking his recipes (he had to account for the fact that the elevation of Jackson is 6,500 feet, which can wreak havoc on baking) and started sending out samples to area restaurants. "Even before we opened we went in and talked with stores and restaurants to see what they were using, asking what they wanted, and then figuring out and sending samples to them," Kevin says. Many of the establishments Kevin and Ali, his wife, approached were still using frozen bread products. When they tasted the difference between what Kevin could provide for them and the frozen items they were willing to give the new bakery a chance. Those initial wholesale accounts gave Kevin the confidence that his bakery was on the right track.

By the time Persephone Bakery officially opened in May it already had signed up a number of wholesale accounts. Kevin wanted to maximize Jackson's short but busy summer season, so he signed up for the town's two weekly farmers' markets as well. "[The farmers' markets] were a good way to get our name out there and a great way to advertise," Kevin says. In fact, other than some small print ads in the local newspaper, Persephone Bakery has built a strong retail and wholesale business for their breads, croissants, custom cakes, and specialty desserts mainly through word-of-mouth marketing. In a town as small as Jackson, those word-of-mouth recommendations are Kevin's strongest marketing tool. "I think it's definitely easier to start a small business in a small town," Kevin says, "in part because the local papers love doing stories about local businesses so it's easier to get your name out than it would be in a large city." Kevin adds that since Jackson has a limited number of local newspapers and magazines, especially when compared to bigger towns or cities, it makes it easier for him to split his advertising budget accordingly and still reach the majority of the population.

But a growing wholesale business, along with two farmers' markets and a special order business, left Persephone Bakery severely understaffed the first few months of business. The business grew so quickly, in fact, that within the first six months of operation it grew from just Kevin and Ali to a staff of five in addition to Kevin and Ali. "I've slept at the bakery before," Kevin admits sheepishly. "We had a hard time finding help at first. Finding someone with experience in this area was impossible so I've had to learn how to manage and train people." Kevin says that the managerial side of the business does not come naturally to him but he's learning how to better communicate with his staff and provide constructive criticism – a task that's made harder by the fact that some of his staff do not speak English as a first language.

Just when Kevin thought he was getting a handle on his new staff he was caught off guard with payroll taxes. Like all U.S. employers, Kevin was required to file payroll taxes with the government. "Truthfully," Kevin admits, "payroll taxes were a term I had heard but I didn't know much about them." Thankfully, with the help of his father and sister, who are both accountants, he was able to quickly get his books in order and make sure that he was paid up with the government. "Accounting is just not in my blood," Kevin says, "but I've since learned how important it is to be on top of that from day one."

Kevin built an office above the bakery along with a small conference room for meetings with clients, but he tries to avoid spending the night at the bakery these days. A normal day for him starts around 4 a.m. and ends around 1 p.m. Days off are few and far between at this early stage of his business' growth. Despite the lack of down time, Kevin says that he finds it really rewarding working for himself. "I'm able to do things the way I want to do them and to see that payoff is a great feeling." And he's still excited about the growth potential of Persephone Bakery. "I would still love to have that little retail space in town," he says. "I think the town could use it. This town needs a nice little middle-of-the-road bakery."

PERSEPHONE BAKERY

RECIPE FOR SUCCESS

 Wait If You Need To. When most people decide they want to start a business they want to get started immediately. Kevin had the foresight to realize that he needed more training to make his business a success. Despite the fact that this required him to move away from the town he loved for several years, when he returned he was better prepared to start and run his bakery than he ever would have been had he stayed and tried to learn it all on his own. While it may be frustrating to put an idea on hold, if your idea is a good one then chances are that shelving it for a few weeks, months, or even years as you better prepare yourself will help set you up for success.

Expect Delays. Kevin's experience building his commercial kitchen shows that it always takes more money and more time than you anticipate. Even if you aren't planning something as large scale as building a commercial kitchen, know that in business you will always come up against delays you didn't anticipate. If at all possible, overestimate how long you think it will take you to get your business up and running so that you aren't caught off guard when delays occur.

Business Is Business. As Kevin realized, the IRS doesn't care that you're a baker and not an accountant. When you start your small business you will be responsible for all aspects of running that business, which includes far more than simply making the product. Make sure that in addition to creating a business plan and marketing strategy, you also understand all the legal and tax responsibilities of the business you're planning to start. Before you make any major changes to your business, including hiring on staff or changing your business structure, you should consult with experts if you have any questions about how this will impact your tax liabilities.

Know What You're Getting Into. The last thing Kevin would have wanted was to put money into starting a bakery only to realize that he wasn't a morning person. If you can, find opportunities that will allow you to experience what working in the food industry is really like. Many people have a romantic notion about opening up a bakery, café, or a farmers' market business and neglect to realize that there is a lot of labor involved. Offer yourself up as cheap help or even volunteer to intern with a local producer to see if this artisan life is for you

Marketing Can Be Local. Marketing that works well in one area may not necessarily work well in another. If you read an article about how well a certain marketing technique worked for one entrepreneur, don't necessarily expect the same results. You have to ask yourself how your target audience likes to receive information in your specific market. While Twitter and Facebook can be great social media tools, in some smaller towns like Jackson, the local newspaper still reigns as the top provider of information to local residents. By focusing his marketing efforts on news mediums that will actually reach his target market, Kevin saves himself time and money.

Learn How To Manage Effectively. Once your business grows to the point where you have to hire on extra hands to help you, you must put on the manager hat and figure out how best to communicate and motivate your staff. Sadly, there's no magic formula to make this step in the process easy, so you have to figure out what works best for each individual that you manage. While your business may be a labor of love for you, to most people it's just a job. It's up to you to make it interesting, fulfilling, or satisfying enough for them so that they give you their best work. At end of the day, they may be helping you produce products, keep your accounting books balanced, or be the ones on the front lines convincing retailers to bring your product into stores, but it's your company's reputation on the line. Make sure that you manage in such a way that whoever you have helping you is living up to the standards you've set for your company.

MOTHER PEACH CARAMELS
BUILD A TEAM OF STRONG SUPPORTERS

As a food journalist for *The Oregonian*, the paper of record for the City of Portland and the largest newspaper in Oregon, Cheri Swoboda was used to seeing her fair share of high-quality artisan products cross her desk. In her 24-year career with the newspaper, she did everything from creating recipes ("30-minute meals were always popular," Cheri says with a laugh) to writing columns on teaching children how to cook. She also wrote articles for the Market Basket section of the newspaper, where she helped introduce new artisan food products and fun kitchen gadgets to *The Oregonian's* readers. She never anticipated she'd switch roles though and be the person in the paper!

As people in office environments are apt to do, Cheri always enjoyed bringing treats she'd made at home into the office to share with her co-workers. Over the years, she gained quite a reputation with the staff for the handmade caramels she'd bring in from time to time. The caramels were from a recipe that Cheri had developed years earlier when, as a 10-year-old, her mother had given her free reign to experiment in the kitchen. "My mother was a fabulous cook," Cheri says, "and she was always very encouraging in letting me try different things in baking and letting me take over her kitchen." One area where Cheri's mother was absolutely the queen of the kitchen though was with her old-fashioned, hand-stirred fudge. Young Cheri was wise enough to know that she shouldn't even try to beat her mother at her own game and decided then she'd let her mother be the master of fudge because she was going to focus on caramels instead.

That focus paid off later, making Cheri a minor celebrity amongst friends, family, and colleagues. Though her main purpose was to give the caramels out as holiday presents and teacher gifts, she would get requests from people wanting to purchase her treats. So Cheri, while working full time at the paper, got her business licenses though she never figured the caramels would amount to much more than a hobby business.

One huge benefit Cheri had in her favor when it came to securing those business licenses is the fact that Oregon has long had a Cottage Food Law in place. This law enables artisan food businesses that produce nonhazardous foods, such as baked goods, to work out of their home kitchen. These kitchens have to be permitted by Oregon's Department of Agriculture and there are basic restrictions -- such as not allowing pets in the kitchen -- but the ability to legally operate an artisan food business from home can save a startup food business a significant amount of money.

In 2008, Cheri found herself caught in a massive shifting of the tides within the newspaper industry. Changing consumer preferences towards online media outlets and vanishing advertising dollars prompted hundred of layoffs and forced retirements across the industry. "I realized that there were no jobs in my industry," Cheri says, "so I decided to take everyone's advice and try to turn my caramels into a full-time business."

With her home kitchen already certified by the Oregon Department of Agriculture, Cheri already had one big piece of the process in place, but that didn't mean she was ready to go to market immediately. "I had a lot of packaging already," Cheri explains, talking about the packaging she had been using when she was simply giving her caramels away as gifts. "My old packaging was more on the folksy side though, and I wanted something more upscale that would look inviting and pristine when sitting on a store shelf."

Cheri started her packaging redesign by walking up and down the aisles of stores, taking note of what packaging she liked and what she didn't. With some rough ideas in mind, Cheri hired a local graphic artist and a local box manufacturing company to help her bring her vision to life. "It was important for me to stay local and add my little piece back to Portland," Cheri says. "I've also found it's easier to work with local people because you can meet them face-to-face and bounce ideas off one another."

Food packaging is more than just a pretty box though and Cheri credits her professional background for helping her understand this. Because she was planning to sell her caramels wholesale to stores as well as through online retail channels, her packaging needed nutritional labels and allergen statements. So Cheri pulled out her Rolodex from her newspaper days and started searching for someone who might be able to direct her to a reputable lab that could perform the necessary testing on her caramels. "Fortunately one of the women I worked with at *The Oregonian* also worked for a company that did nutritional fact labels," she says.

Cheri could have conducted the nutritional analysis on her own with the help of online software, but felt it was important to work with a professional and recommends other food entrepreneurs do the same. "If you're going to put that much money into packaging," Cheri says, "and it will have your name and your label on it then it only makes sense to go with a professional company. They know how many ounces is considered a serving, how many pieces are in a serving, etc." Allergen statements also are particularly important for food entrepreneurs developing packaging. It's vital that allergen statements are accurate so as to prevent someone with a life-threatening food allergy from mistakenly eating anything that would harm them. "From milk, to nuts, to gluten intolerance," Cheri says, "those are the things that are probably the most difficult and the hardest to make sure they are precisely done for food products, and that's where a professional can be a huge help."

Another challenge for Cheri was figuring out where she was going to store all these boxes for her caramels. Her boxes, like most custom packaging, get less expensive on a per-unit basis when she purchases more of them at a time. While it would be ideal to purchase the maximum number of boxes her business bank account would allow, the reality was she didn't have room for thousands of boxes in her home. Cheri had to figure out how many boxes she could order without turning her entire house into a packaging plant. Thanks to the collaborative relationship with both her graphic artist and the box manufacturer, the team decided the easiest solution would be a box that ships flat and is manually assembled prior to adding the caramels and shipping to customers. This allows Cheri the ability to enjoy a price break by ordering in bulk without turning her entire home into warehouse for caramel packaging.

Even with that price break for ordering in bulk, Cheri soon learned the lesson that many artisan food entrepreneurs learn: quality packaging can be prohibitively expensive, especially on a tight startup budget. Partway through the packaging redesign process for her traditional caramels, Cheri realized that the best use of her financial resources was to go ahead and design and manufacture a box for her chocolate caramels, too. Even though there would be two different box designs, it still would help lower her per-unit packaging cost. At that time though, Cheri hadn't yet perfected her chocolate caramel recipe, so she threw herself into recipe testing mode and, when she had a product she was happy with, rushed the chocolate caramels to the lab for nutritional testing.

During another meeting with her designer and box manufacturer, Cheri happened to mention that she thought it would be great to offer a sampler pack for people to try. Her idea, she explained, was to put some caramels in a bag and tie it with a bow. "The great thing about working with people who are local is that you can brainstorm with them and they can give you immediate feedback," Cheri says. "I happened to mention the sampler box idea to my box guy and he said 'I think I have the perfect box for you." The box design he showed her was just the right size for five to six Mother Peach Caramels and, with a lower price point, offered the customer the opportunity to order a sample batch of caramels to try rather than committing to a half-pound or pound of caramels. The sample pack also turned out to be a great inexpensive gift for realtors to give to their clients and Cheri has rapidly built up a realtor business she hadn't originally considered.

All told, it took Cheri approximately nine months to get her caramels ready to sell. That is partly due to the time she spent developing the packaging and perfecting the chocolate caramel recipe, but also because Cheri didn't want to rush to market and make any big or expensive mistakes along the way. During those nine months, she frequently went back to her Rolodex and connected with people she knew through *The Oregonian* and other food entrepreneurs, some of whom she'd once featured in the paper, to hear about their experiences in the food industry. "You have to be bold enough to find another company or two and offer to take them to coffee and ask for help," Cheri recommends for other aspiring food entrepreneurs. "Most people are more than helpful and they are very kind and very nice about doing it. You just can't be afraid to ask questions."

All her planning paid off. Within a month of her website going live, Cheri received an invitation to participate in ChocolateFest with her chocolate caramels. This event has historically attracted more than 10,000 chocophiles, so Cheri knew that this was a great opportunity to spread the word about her new company. Because of the event's focus on chocolate items, she also knew that she needed a chocolate-specific samples box for the event. "I immediately called up my box guy and we added a chocolate sampler-size box." Cheri also worked closely with her box manufacturer to develop a two-piece taster box as well, which has proven to be a hit for gift baskets, coffee stores, wedding clients, and the hospitality industry as thank-you gifts to their customers.

The two-piece taster box also has turned out to be a great sales vehicle to help Cheri grow her business. The taster box allows store employees to test Cheri's wares before putting them in front of customers. Starting with stores in the Portland area, Cheri put together her own sales package with a press release, pricing, and, most importantly of all, samples of her caramels, and dropped them off around town. "This has been very successful for me," Cheri says. "I also try to think of people I know and reach out to them and drop off a sample. It helps me leapfrog over the gatekeepers whose job it is to say no."

Having worked at *The Oregonian* for so many years, Cheri also didn't hesitate to approach her former colleagues and ask them to feature her company in the paper. As so many of her former co-workers were already fans of Cheri's caramels, they were happy to oblige. Three weeks before Christmas, Mother Peach Caramels were featured in the paper's popular FOODday column. That type of publicity and exposure helped get Mother Peach Caramels' name in front of thousands of potential customers and led to a rush of orders that has rarely slowed down since.

As Mother Peach Caramels grows in popularity, Cheri knows that it will one day outgrow the confines of her home kitchen. "I've even looked at a couple different buildings and snooped to see how much it is a square foot," she admits. "At this point, though, I'm still home-based and I'm still able to get both cars in the garage even with four pallets of boxes in our garage!"

www.motherpeachcaramels.com

Tap Into Your Network. Cheri's 20 years of experience as a food journalist allowed her to tap into a unique network of experts and colleagues when starting her business. But just because you don't have the same background doesn't mean that you can't be successful. Use your network to its fullest to help your business succeed. This includes letting everyone you know about your company and don't be afraid to ask for any introductions to key people your friends and family may know. By using tools like Facebook and LinkedIn, we're now all truly only separated by six degrees of separation, if even that much, so you may be surprised by how often your network will be able to help you out.

Ask Questions. Having a strong network in place is one thing, but you need to be willing to ask questions. Most people are more than happy to help you and want to see you succeed, but they don't know how to help you if you don't ask. Once again, Cheri's experience as a journalist left her uniquely suited to this task but this is a characteristic you should cultivate in yourself because it will serve you and your business well.

Think Long-term. Your business may be in the initial stages right now, but things like your company name, your packaging, and your product portfolio are items that will be with your company for a very long time. By taking that long-term approach, Cheri was able to work with a packaging designer to develop packaging that could suit her needs for years to come. Rather than simply trying to solve for the immediate problem, take a look down the road and ask yourself where you see your business going so you can make decisions that will help you both today and in the future.

Minimize Costs When Possible. Starting a small food business, even one out of your own home, can be costly. As an artisan food entrepreneur, whether you're just starting up or looking to grow your existing business, you need to keep a tight rein on expenses. One way Cheri accomplishes this is by purchasing her packaging in bulk, which enables her to get a lower price per piece. While this does require a larger one-time upfront cost for all the packaging, it serves the purpose of lowering her overall costs. That means she makes a little more money every time she sells a box of caramels. As you weigh one decision over another, don't be too quick to take the cheaper option if an investment now will lower your costs across the board.

Outsource Locally. When it comes to hiring outside talent, like a graphic artist or web developer, to assist you with your business, it may be tempting to go with the lowest bidder regardless of their location. But there are some substantial benefits to hiring someone local. The biggest of these, especially for projects that are creative in nature, is the ability to meet with the contractor face-to-face to clearly convey what vision you have for the project and to brainstorm ideas. While this can be accomplished via a telephone call or e-mail discussion, there sometimes is no substitute for meeting in person. And, as Cheri points out, staying local puts money back into your own local economy. In many cases these are the people you want buying your products, so shouldn't you support them in their endeavors as well? Not to mention, someone local also is more likely to share your company's name with their local friends and family as well, which could result in even more sales for you.

CONCLUSION

As evidenced through the experiences shared by the entrepreneurs in this book, starting a business, specifically an artisan food business, has its fair share of hurdles. What's more, those challenges don't simply disappear once your business is up and running. The problems themselves may change but part of your role as an entrepreneur is to work through the issues that arise and try to turn them into opportunities for your business.

Throughout this book we've taken a look at the many different ways entrepreneurs overcome the obstacles that the "middle" of their business' life cycle throws their way. In conducting these interviews I noted that despite these different approaches, each of these entrepreneurs have several key attributes in common. It would be brazen to say that these alone are the keys to entrepreneurial success but, at the very least, these personality traits will serve you well as you guide your business through its start-up and middle phases and grow it into a company worthy of its own success story.

Passion For Their Product. No matter how glamorous a culinary career may seem to an outsider, those in the kitchen day-in and day-out know that being a food entrepreneur can be grueling, backbreaking, tiresome work. Every food entrepreneur I've ever spoken with either knows this before jumping into the field or quickly learns it once they've put their feet in the fire. That being said, the hard work, long hours, and erratic paychecks aren't a deterrent to these folks. At their core, these food entrepreneurs love what they're doing and they literally pour their heart and soul into the products they make. Theirs is not a production game in which they aim to churn out as many widgets as they can to maximize profit. These entrepreneurs slave over their products and want to make sure that everything that goes out the door with their name on it will bring joy to a customer. Passion like that is not easy to sustain over a long period of time unless it is genuine and for each of these entrepreneurs that is certainly the case.

[117]

sire For More. The people featured in these pages, and other trepreneurs I've spoken with throughout the years, aren't the typ no would be happy punching a clock every day for the rest of their lives. They believe that they have the capacity to create something – a product, a business, a life – that is different from the norm, and they believe that the benefits inherent with going out on their own will, at the end of the day, outweigh the risks. It's not always easy to jump off that ledge and hope that your dreams will catch you on the other side. In many cases, starting off in a part-time capacity may be your best move until you feel comfortable taking that next step. For those who dare to act on their dreams the rewards can be substantial.

Building On Their Background. Many food entrepreneurs come into this industry having worked in other jobs and other fields. High-end chefs may spend their whole lives dreaming of one day running a Michelin-rated restaurant, but artisan food entrepreneurs are just as likely to have been working on Wall Street or driving a cab before deciding to give it all up and start over with a handful of recipes and a spatula as their guide. Even if it seems as though your background has no relation to the food business you'd like to start, keep in mind that any experience you bring to the table is likely to prove helpful along the way. Becoming a food entrepreneur is not just about the food; your business skills are a critical ingredient too. As an entrepreneur you are going to have to wear every hat in the office so any skills and experience you've cultivated in other careers will be assets in this one.

A Humble Attitude. We've met food entrepreneurs who used to enjoy corner offices and who once considered ties and heels a mandatory part of their work wardrobe. Transitioning into food entrepreneurs, those who succeed are those who are able to put their former titles aside and get the work done – regardless of what needs to be done. It doesn't matter who you were in your former professional life, when it comes to your business you will be the one responsible for the unglamorous tasks such as doing the dishes and taking out the trash at the end of the day. That doesn't mean these entrepreneurs don't have big plans for their businesses, they just recognize that in order to achieve great things they have to be willing to put in the work no matter how tedious or dirty it may seem.

Knack For Problem Solving. Food entrepreneurs don't typically have a large staff to turn to when a problem arises, and when it's your business, it seems like every day there's a new problem or question in need of an immediate answer. Those artisan food entrepreneurs who are able to not only work through these issues, but who actually seem to relish the challenges that are thrown at them, are the best suited to succeed over the long-term. The truth of the matter is that no matter how big or small your company there will always be problems that need to be solved, and when you're the boss, it's your job to make those decisions. The beauty of owning your own business is that you can decide how creative you want to be in solving those issues, and you don't have to fight through layers of red tape to get the job done. To the right person problem-solving is an exhilarating part of business ownership. It is what seperates business owners who never make it past the start-up stage from those who manage to build the business they always dreamed of.

ACKNOWLEDGEMENTS

This may go without saying, but this book would not have been possible without Mari Luangrath of Foiled Cupcakes, Lea Richards of Pig Of The Month, Lori and Michelle Corso of Twin Cakes Bakery, Jennie Broderick of Sassy Sweet Treats, Tom Gallo and Susan Devitt of GalloLea Organics, Rebeca Krones and Luis Zevallos of Tropical Traders Specialty Foods, Kevin and Ali Cohane of Persephone Bakery, and Cheri Swoboda of Mother Peach Caramels. Each of these very busy food artisans gave generously of their time to answer the questions I posed about their businesses and provided feedback throughout the many months it took to write this book. It should be noted that the businesses highlighted in this book represent some of the very best food and business practices in today's growing artisan food industry. With minimal resources, when compared to the mass-manufactured food products they compete against, these food artisans are committed to creating the very best possible products and helping re-teach consumers that real food – that which is made with real ingredients and not chemicals – is how we as human beings were meant to eat. Please note, any mistakes in this book are my own and are not representative of the companies featured here.

I must also thank Tamara Miller who took her red pen to this manuscript to weed out poor punctuation, misspellings, and weak sentence structure. Her expertise is, as always, invaluable, and I am grateful for her time and her friendship.

Michelle Draeger of mdraeger designs is the only graphic artist I trust with my book covers as she's been the brain and talent behind all three book jackets thus far. She is always eager and excited to tackle the projects I send her and I am truly lucky to have her artistic eye on my side.

Zoe-Ann Bartlett continues to be my biggest cheerleader in everything I do. I don't know where I'd be without her friendship, guidance, and plethora of ideas. In almost every case, the advice she's given me has always been right on target. Now if only I would start listening!

Without my family I would be nowhere. My poor parents are by now used to receiving late night e-mails from me asking which book title they like better and whether one cover image is better than another. They always provide me with quick and honest feedback and unwavering support and for that I am grateful.

My loving husband continues to provide me with the necessary emotional support as I venture into uncharted waters with each new book. He provides guidance when asked and, perhaps even more importantly, picks up the responsibilities of home and hearth when I go on a writing binge, so thank you a hundred times over.

And, as always, the last acknowledgements are reserved for Greta and Tyr for being the lights of my life.

15293440R00066

Made in the USA
Lexington, KY
18 May 2012